Pearson

T0385896

Year **3**

Handwriting
Activity Workbook

Horse

Horse

Home learning from the experts

Author:

Sarah Loader

About this book

This book supports the practice and consolidation of handwriting skills, with lots of engaging, fun activities to help children grow in confidence and ability.

Clear, consistent, cursive handwriting is not only a statutory requirement of the English curriculum, but is the gateway to success in all subjects. The ability to present ideas legibly and clearly is a critical life skill.

Handwriting made clear

- Handwriting requires strong fine-motor skills and pencil control. The tasks in this activity book develop and refine those skills.
- Key skills are learned and reinforced through a wide range of tasks to keep children engaged and interested in each activity.
- Helpful tips and reminders support children as they work.

How to use this book

- Little-and-often is a productive approach to handwriting, as it requires great concentration and can be frustrating. Children can work through just one or two activities in a sitting, and stop when they lose interest to avoid it becoming negative.
- Try to complete the activities in the given order, as they progress in challenge and expectation.
- Your child will ideally work through activities independently, but it's worth being there for when support is needed.
- Explore the Progress Points with your child as they work through the book to see where further support is needed.

Getting started

- Make your child's learning space interesting and fun.
- Encourage your child to step away from any technology or energetic games a little while beforehand, and to take some deep breaths to help them focus.
- Make sure your child is holding their pencil properly.
- Sit with your child to start with, even if you're occupied with your own task.

Challenges to overcome

Making handwriting consistent with equal spaces between words
As children write more, the challenge is in making it consistent, so their letters all sit on the right place on the line, are in proportion with each other, and the spaces between each word are roughly the same. Reminding children to look back at their own writing is important for developing their awareness of this.

Using neat, cursive writing regularly

By Year 3 children are generally expected to use cursive handwriting throughout, and keeping this neat can be tricky until children become more familiar with the joins and the new shapes that cursive writing requires, so practice is key.

Get creative

- To enable longer handwriting practice, children could write a letter to you or to someone else. The response could inspire a continuing exchange.
- Children could create an advert – for example about a place they've visited or their favourite toy – to keep practising the organisation of text as well as their handwriting.
- Children could write an information text or fact-file about something they're interested in – again practising text organisation alongside handwriting.
- Try finding an advert in a magazine or newspaper and ask children to create a poster or a fact-file from the information.

National curriculum coverage

As well as covering the Year 3 handwriting statutory requirements, this activity book develops and practises handwriting skills within the context of the wider English curriculum, so that tasks and activities are meaningful and relevant for children. Some of these objectives are taken from the previous year as useful revision.

Topic	Curriculum relevance
Homophones	English Appendix 1: Spelling (work for Years 3 and 4)
Prefixes	English Appendix 1: Spelling (work for Years 3 and 4)
Spellings with ci, cy, ce, se	English Appendix 1: Spelling (work for Year 2)
Suffixes	English Appendix 1: Spelling (work for Years 3 and 4)
Punctuation	English Appendix 2: Vocabulary, grammar and punctuation (work for Year 2)
Present and past tense	English Appendix 2: Vocabulary, grammar and punctuation (work for Year 2)
Direct speech	Writing – Vocabulary, grammar and punctuation (Years 3 and 4 Programme of Study)
Organising paragraphs around a theme	Writing – Composition (Years 3 and 4 Programme of Study)
Using headings and sub-headings	Writing – Composition (Years 3 and 4 Programme of Study)

Activity 1

Use the words in the box to complete the sentences in the letter, using each word only once! Remember to join your letters together.

safe dishonest perilous important fortunate
before completely poisoned traitors forbidden

Dear Lord Cole,

I am ___fortunate___ to be writing this letter,

as we are _____ from doing so.

But I must be careful as I am being watched.

It is very _____ that as soon as you

have read it, you destroy it, _____

anyone else reads it. There are _____

in the castle. No one can be trusted, everyone is

_____ and it is _____

here. You must get a message to the King. For him to

be _____ he must get rid of anyone he

cannot _____ trust, starting with the

chefs, before we are all _____ .

Yours sincerely, Sir Simon

Activity 2

Write out the sentences, choosing the correct homophone to complete each one.

Homophones are words that sound the same, but have different spellings and meanings.

1. It's (grate / great) when we have football at school.

_____

2. They tried to (berry / bury) the treasure.

_____

3. I (mist / missed) the bus again.

_____

4. I love it when Eskil and I (meat / meet) in the park.

_____

5. I definitely told her to come (here / hear).

_____

6. Don't eat that red (berry / bury).

_____

7. I didn't (here / hear) Mum calling.

_____

8. The (mist / missed) lay low over the fields.

_____

Activity 3

Draw lines to match the beginnings to these words and write out each word in full. Then write a sentence of your own using one of the words.

The add-ons at the beginning of words are called prefixes.

dis	appoint	_disappoint_
	behave	_____
	happy	_____
mis	fair	_____
	obey	_____
	agree	_____
in	active	_____
	correct	_____
un	spell	_____
	lock	_____

It is <u>unfair</u> that my sister gets away with so much!

_____

_____

Activity 4

Write out the sentences, choosing the correct word from the box to complete each one.

disagree   misspell   unhappy   misbehave
incorrect   disobey   unfair

1. It is ___?___ that I can't stay up late.

    _____

2. I often ___?___ with my parents about TV.

    _____

3. It is easy to ___?___ my name.

    _____

4. You get into trouble if you ___?___ the rules.

    _____

5. I often feel ___?___ on a Sunday.

    _____

6. I hate getting ___?___ answers in tests.

    _____

7. Mum warned us not to ___?___ .

    _____

Activity 5

Write out the sentences, choosing the correct homophone to complete each one.

1. The teacher told us to get some (plain / plane) paper.

   _____

2. It is (not / knot) nice to be unkind.

   _____

3. I had never (scene / seen) Grandpa look so happy!

   _____

4. I'm not sure (weather / whether) or not he's coming.

   _____

5. I was only allowed one (peace / piece) of cake.

   _____

6. The (not / knot) was very hard to untie.

   _____

7. The (weather / whether) was warm all summer.

   _____

 I can write more homophones.

Activity 6

Write out the sentences, choosing the correct word from the box to complete each one.

cycling   city   tricycle   house
mouse   centre   nurse

1. The ____?____ at the hospital was very kind.

    _____

2. We have lived in our ____?____ for two years.

    _____

3. The ____?____ centre is busy and noisy.

    _____

4. I have a new pet ____?____ .

    _____

5. My little sister rides a ____?____ .

    _____

6. I love ____?____ to school.

    _____

7. We met Nana at the shopping ____?____ .

    _____

2 I can write words with ci, cy, ce and se spellings.

Activity 7

Draw lines to match the beginnings to these words and write out each word in full. Then write a sentence of your own using one of the words.

possible   _____

patient   _____

im   regular   _____

merge   _____

ir   appear   _____

decorate   _____

sub   turn   _____

marine   _____

re   heading   _____

responsible   _____

divide   _____

I have always wanted to go in a <u>submarine</u>.

_____

_____

Activity 8

Write out the sentences, choosing the correct word from the box to complete each one.

irregular submarine sub-heading impatient
irresponsible redecorate return

1. I'm very _____?_____ waiting for the bus.

   _____

2. The trains can be terribly _____?_____.

   _____

3. Mum says we need to _____?_____ the kitchen.

   _____

4. Don't forget to use a _____?_____ in your writing.

   _____

5. What time will you _____?_____ from the cinema?

   _____

6. The _____?_____ headed out to sea.

   _____

7. Those two are so _____?_____ when they go out.

   _____

Activity 9

Write out a timetable, choosing one or more activities from the list for each day of the week. You can repeat activities!

Activities

Tennis lesson   Dog walk   Running club
School assembly   Choir practice   Swimming class
Cleaning my bedroom   Homework

Day	Activities
Monday	Running club, Dog walk

Activity 10

Write out the months of the year. Remember to begin each month with a capital letter.

Make sure all your letters sit neatly on the line.

January   _____

February   _____

March   _____

April   _____

May   _____

June   _____

July   _____

August   _____

September   _____

October   _____

November   _____

December   _____

3 I can write the months of the year.

Activity 11

Draw lines to match the beginnings to these words and write out each word in full. Then write a sentence of your own using one of the words.

market _____

septic _____

super

clockwise _____

graph _____

inter

star _____

man _____

anti

social _____

biography _____

auto

city _____

national _____

I have the goalkeeper's <u>autograph</u>.

_____

_____

Activity 12

Write out the sentences, choosing the correct word from the box to complete each one.

supermarket antisocial autobiography antiseptic
international anticlockwise

1. We were told to run in an ____?____ direction.

   _____

2. We go to the ____?____ every Saturday.

   _____

3. Mum put ____?____ on my sore knee.

   _____

4. Jan has done a lot of ____?____ travel.

   _____

5. Have you read that footballer's ____?____ ?

   _____

6. I felt really ____?____ at the party.

   _____

4 I can write words with prefixes.

Activity 13

There is no punctuation in this text. Rewrite it, adding in commas, full stops and capital letters. Remember to join your letters together.

when i looked out of the window this morning it was pouring with rain but that doesn't bother me there's loads you can do in the rain like jumping in puddles making enormous splashes with your bike and getting really muddy mum gets cross about the state my clothes get in but it's worth it

When I looked _____

_____

_____

_____

_____

_____

_____

_____

Activity 14

Write a sentence about an activity you can do in each season, or use the activities in the box for your sentences. Use full sentences and remember to join your letters together.

<u>Activities</u>
Build a snowman
Collect leaves and conkers
Swim in the sea
Look at the newborn lambs

Spring _In Spring I like to_ _____

_____

Summer _____

_____

Autumn _____

_____

Winter _____

_____

Activity 15

Write the months of the year under the correct season.
Remember to begin each month with a capital letter.
Then add the correct sentence for each season and draw
a picture.

In Autumn, I like jumping in muddy puddles.

In Spring, I enjoy looking at all the daffodils.

In Winter, I love being cosy at home.

In Summer, I love eating ice cream!

Spring

March _____

_____

_____

In Spring, _____

Summer

June

_____

_____

Autumn

September

_____

_____

Winter

December

_____

_____

Activity 16

Draw lines to match the endings to these words and write out each word in full. Then write a sentence of your own using one of the words.

You may need to take away the last letter of the root word.

admire _admiration_

sad _____

poison _____

ous

inform _____

final _____

ation

prepare _____

fame _____

ly

usual _____

mountain _____

danger _____

We were full of <u>admiration</u> for the athlete.

_____

_____

Activity 17

Write out the sentences, choosing the correct word from the box to complete each one.

> information admiration famous sadly
> furious usually mountainous

1. Kat walked away ____?____ .

   _____

2. That area of the country is very ____?____ .

   _____

3. She was ____?____ before joining the band.

   _____

4. I've got lots of ____?____ for my parents.

   _____

5. I got ____?____ about the concert online.

   _____

6. I'm ____?____ late for the bus.

   _____

7. My brother was cross, but my sister was ____?____ .

   _____

Activity 18

You have found this letter in a bottle washed up on the beach, but it is wet. Rewrite it in your best handwriting.

SOS! I have washed ashore on a small island, and am badly hurt. I need you to try to find me as the island is extremely dangerous. It is very mountainous and there are vicious monkeys and enormous tigers. I am trying to be courageous, but please, make your preparations, and come quickly.

_____

_____

_____

_____

_____

_____

_____

5 I can write words with suffixes.

Activity 19

Rewrite the text, putting it into the past tense.

I love school. The best bit is all the different subjects – so you can always find something you like. There are quite a few practical subjects – like DT and Dance, and of course PE, which is my absolute favourite. But the best bit? Break time of course, when I just sit about with my friends, chatting, laughing and generally chilling!

I loved school.

6 I can write in the past tense.

Activity 20

Complete the sentences using the text from the speech bubbles.

Remember to use opening and closing speech marks.

Don't forget your packed lunch!

_____

_____ said Mum.

Come in from the garden, Callum!

Dad called, _____

_____

What time do you call this?

Bee looked at her watch. _____

_____ she said.

Do you want an ice cream?

_____

_____ Gran asked.

I'm soaked! That's the last football game I go to!

_____

_____

_____

_____ Hal said, laughing.

Activity 21

Rewrite the text adding in speech marks in the right places to show the dialogue.

Remember to start each person's dialogue on a new line.

Albe, are you home? I called. Hi Mum, we're in here, Albe said eventually. Hasif, Gemma, Danny! You're all here, I said. I did tell you that I was having friends round, Mum, Albe replied. It's ok, isn't it? Of course! I said, smiling. Who wants snacks? I asked. Yes please! they all shouted.

"Albe, are you home?" I called.

_____

_____

_____

_____

_____

_____

_____

_____

7 I can use speech marks.

Activity 22

Read the text and write a summary sentence or two in your best handwriting for each paragraph.

The Big Match

Tensions were running high on Saturday afternoon as the two big rivals met on the pitch for the first time in seven years. Who would be champions? As each team had the same number of wins behind them, it was anybody's guess. Fans piled into the stadium for the match of the decade.

A Flying Start

Both teams looked ready for the challenge as they ran onto the pitch. As soon as the whistle blew they were off and a goal was scored within two minutes.

2–0

Before half-time there was another goal taking the score to 2–0, and giving one team a clear advantage. As the players jogged off the pitch, there was jubilation at one end of the stadium and disappointment at the other.

A hat-trick

Everything changed after half-time, when the losing team came out fighting and with fresh energy. They dominated and within 20 minutes the striker had scored two goals. Then, with five minutes to go, another goal, a hat-trick for the striker and a win for his team.

Paragraph 1: _Two rival teams met for the first time in_

seven years.

Paragraph 2:

Paragraph 3:

Paragraph 4:

Is your handwriting looking neat and tidy?

Activity 23

Rewrite this poster about a missing dog. To make it eye-catching, use headings and only include the most important information. You could also draw a picture of the missing dog.

Missing: Our dog Amy.

Age: 4½ years old.

Likes: Cuddles, a warm fire and plenty of food – she's not fussy!

Dislikes: Loud noises, shouting, fireworks.

Missing for three days.

Amy is a black and white sheepdog. She has a white stripe down the middle of her face and the tip of her tail is white. She comes when she is called, but can be nervous around strangers. She often hides behind bins where she scavenges for food.

We really miss her and want her back.

If you see Amy around town, please call the Wesley family on 61082 574913.

MISSING!

_____

_____

_____

_____

_____

_____

_____

_____

_____

8 I can use headings to organise text.

Activity 24

Rewrite the information text about mountaineering, adding in paragraph breaks and choosing headings from the box.

> Mountaineering   Equipment
> What to take   Safety first
> Know your environment   Have fun!

Mountaineering is a fun, exciting activity, but it can be dangerous so you must be careful. Always make sure you take the right equipment with you: ropes, maps, wet-weather clothing, good shoes, a torch and a phone. Make sure you have plenty of supplies with you: for example, extra clothing, lots of food and water. Don't go mountaineering alone, so, if something happens, there is someone who can go for help. Do your research before setting out so you know what to expect. If you've prepared properly, you'll have an amazing time, so have fun!

9 I can use paragraphs to organise text.

Mountaineering

My name is _____